The Booming Boots of Joey Jones

David Clayton

Illustrated by Stephen Player

OXFORD
UNIVERSITY PRESS

CHAPTER 1

Joe feels lucky

Joey Jones was a laugh, everyone knew that. He didn't really mean to be funny. He was just a one-man disaster zone. No matter how many times he tried to succeed, something always seemed to go wrong.

Joe thought about it a lot. Was he clumsy or just unlucky? Sometimes he wondered. Maybe there was always some banana skin out there ready to trip him. Joe didn't know.

It was like the time he messed things up for Tank at the inter-schools swimming gala. Tank was a good swimmer and was winning the free-style final. But Tank just had to be in the outside lane. And Joe just had to go mad and lean over too far just as he trod on his slippery goggles.

Tank wasn't expecting to be dive-bombed. Their meeting ten metres from the finish was the highlight of the evening. The kids laughed. The parents laughed. Even the teachers laughed. Tank did not laugh. Joe never heard the last of his blunder. Tank never forgot that Joe had made him look a fool.

However, just before Christmas, Joe got his chance. He had, at long last, got on to the school football team, and football was king at Newton Hall.

It happened like this. His school was due to play Flowery Field in the cup semi-finals. But there was a problem. Newton was the smallest school in the area. There was always a bit of a gap to fill if anyone was off, as they had so few players to choose from. Now, to make things worse, flu had struck and half the kids were missing.

A week before the game, on practice day, Mr Murphy told Joe the good news.

He bounced into the changing room grinning.

'I'm lucky! So very, very lucky!' Joe said to himself.

The teacher looked carefully at Joe – at his wide grin and big boots.

'We really need you, Joe,' he said. 'But no muck-ups, eh?'

'I won't let you down, sir!' said the boy.

Tank, the team captain, scowled.
'What do we want him for?' he
muttered. 'He's rubbish!'
But Joe's luck had changed. Or had it?

As they went out into the afternoon gloom, he had a good look at the team. It was all odds and ends like a box of liquorice allsorts.

There was speedy little Eddy Morgan, big fat Arthur who almost filled his goal, and red-faced Tank with legs like sausages. Joe noticed, too, that even his skinny friend, Skenner Skelly, was playing for the first time.

The girls doing gymnastics in the hall sniggered at the ragged army as it set out into the sleet. They were in the warm.

However, nothing bothered Joe. He would have played at midnight at the North Pole for a chance like this. So out he ran, on to the school pitch as if it were Wembley. He imagined the crowd chanting, 'Joe-ee! Joe-ee! Joe-ee!' He could smell the velvet turf and hear the singing. 'Joe-ee! Joe-ee!' he muttered to himself, making his own crowd noises.

Mr Murphy watched him from a distance, shook his head and sighed. Then cold air froze his knees and icy water turned his toes to ice cubes and the teacher's heart began to sink. Maybe playing Joe was a mistake?

'Play wide on the left wing, Joe,' said Mr Murphy. 'Don't come inside unless I tell you.'

Joe jogged out towards the motorway fence and the game started. One half of the team played against the other. Sken ended up on the opposite side from Joe.

Joe slipped and slid up and down the wing but he never got a pass, nor did Sken. Just give me one shot, thought Joey. Just one. In his mind he could see the ball fly like a bullet from his boot. He imagined how it would flash away and *smack!* hit the back of the net.

After twenty minutes, Joe knew that he would never get a pass, let alone a shot. In the end, he got fed up. I'm going in the middle, he thought. I'll have a better chance of a shot there. So off he went. There was nothing to lose.

His team was attacking down the right. Eddy Morgan ran past a defender and was going to centre. Joe imagined the ball coming towards him. He thought about it flying off his head low into the net. He could already hear the crowd cheering …

'Joe!' Eddy shouted.

The ball was screaming towards him but it was much too high and fast. If only he had stayed where he was! Too late! Joe tried to jump but his worn boots let him down. The ball hit him on the head like an icy snowball, smashing him down in the sludge before flying out of play.

Eddy came racing over to put his flat nose and skinhead close to Joe's face.

'Why weren't you out there where you were supposed to be?' he snarled. 'You mucked it up!'

Joe just shrugged, 'I … just …'

Eddy grunted like a chimp and stomped off. Joe walked away with a headache and a painful lump.

'I think that's enough for today, lads!' shouted Mr Murphy.

The light was now bad. Joe walked off slowly, whistling to cheer himself up.

'Do you have to whistle?' asked Tank.

'No,' said Joe. 'Why? Is it unlucky?'

'It is when you're whistling,' snapped Tank. 'It means that you're on the team.'

'Leave it out!' Arthur, the big keeper, cut in.

'He's as much use as a chocolate teapot,' growled Tank in disgust. Eddy and Tank walked away muttering.

'I can do this,' Joe said to himself. 'I can! If only I had proper boots. If only the others passed to me. If only it wasn't so dark!'

Skenner came up to Joe as he went into the changing room and peered at him in the darkness.

'I shouldn't have missed it!' groaned Joe.

'Don't worry, Joe,' he said. 'You looked all right to me.'

Joe wasn't fooled. It was a bad miss.

CHAPTER 2

Practice makes perfect

That night Joe did not hang around to chat. As he left, he had one last look at the muddy field lit by the hall lights. Then he walked away from the school. Soon it vanished behind the green mist.

Inside, the *boom-boom-boom* of feet told Joe that the gymnastics hadn't finished. However, he wasn't interested. He only had eyes for the football pitch.

Soon he was passing Ashton's Sports, its windows lined with gleaming football boots. Joe whistled when he saw the prices. There was no chance of buying any.

His mum and dad were saving for a holiday. Christmas wasn't far off either. There was no money to chuck around. No money, no boots.

Still, he could dream, couldn't he? Feel their softness round his toes? Smell their new leather? Tank owned three pairs. Joe heard him talking about them.

Finally, Joe jogged away through the chill and soon he was home.

'Everything all right?' said his mum.

'Oh, yes, Mum. I'm playing football for the school next week.'

'For the school?' coughed his dad, almost dropping his paper. 'I'm so pleased, Joe!'

I've got to do well, thought Joe.
Got to.

That night he went slowly upstairs to
his room. There, posters of his idols
smiled down on him – all strikers.

He stared at them and, as he did, his
mind started floating away. He was
dancing past people, doing overhead
kicks and leaving defenders for dead.

'Yehhh!' he yelled, punching the air as he scored another daydream winner – and knocked the lampshade down.

Crump! The door opened.

'Drink, Joe?' smiled his mum, standing in the doorway with a steaming mug of tea in a Manchester United cup.

His face was hotter than the brew. He booted the fallen shade under the bed. Would she notice the bare light? Mum said nothing.

What a dreamer he was! When Mum had gone he looked in the mirror. He looked at his black hair sprouting like a lavatory brush, his long arms and legs and his huge kipper feet.

'Come on, Joe!' he said to himself, 'do it!'

He had a week in which to practise, a week in which to sort himself out.

Next day, Tank and Eddie started joking about the missed header.

'What wears water-skis, has two shoulders but no head? Joey Jones!'

'What's the difference between Joey Jones and a calendar? A calendar knows what day it is!' and so on.

'How many did you score, Tank?' was all Joe said. Tank scowled.

At the end of the day, he went home. He told his mum he wanted a late tea, got changed and went off to Peel Park alone with his football.

'Having a game with the lads?' asked his dad as he went out.

'No, Dad. It's just me tonight. The others can't make it,' he lied.

When he got there, the place was empty and sad. There was just him and the hulking lines of trees, looming like ghosts in the gloom.

At first, he stomped around, booting the ball up and down, scuffing up the yellow leaves. *Thud! Thud!* He could run all right and give the ball a good crack but it felt like messing around. If only I knew what I was doing wrong, he thought. I'm sure I could do better.

He found a place where there were two trees just about as wide as a goal. Behind them was a high wall. Here he could practise without having to run too far for the ball after each shot.

Great! Now he cracked the ball as hard as he could. Right, left, right, left. When he hit the mark he could hear that Wembley crowd chanting, 'Joe! Joe! Joe!' The trouble was he missed the target ten times as often as he hit it. Then he could hear those same crowds booing and chanting, 'You're-a-load-of-rubbish!'

What was wrong? The slippery boots didn't help.

After another half-hour, the mist was drifting like snow across the park, the trees were black towers, and Joe was worn out.

Suddenly he saw two figures standing in the fog. People were watching.

'Don't stop,' said a familiar voice.

'Yes,' said the taller figure, 'perhaps we can join you?'

'Sken! Mr Skelly?' gasped Joe, amazed. Sken and his dad were standing there. 'What are you doing here?'

Skenner coughed. 'Well, I'm no good but … I don't like Tank laughing at me. We thought we'd have a kick-about. Fancy a game?'

Suddenly, Joe didn't feel alone any more. Suddenly, energy surged through his body.

'Yes, great! I'd really like to,' replied Joe. 'I want to practise. I want to show Tank too.'

First one lad then the other had a go at beating Mr Skelly who was in goal.

Sken was accurate with his shots but he didn't have power. Big Joe thumped it hard but hit the ball all over the place.

'Hang on!'

Sken's dad brought the practice to a halt.

'Let's see you kick a dead ball,' he said to Joe. 'Take a penalty.'

Joe didn't let on how tired he was and had a go. The ball flashed past the man in a blur – but it missed the goal.

'What a shot!' Mr Skelly said. 'But you look up as you kick the ball. That's why it's going wide.'

'I can hardly stand up in these things!' Joe pointed to his great battered boots.

'Forget the boots! Keep your eye on the ball.'

Whap! Joe took a mighty crack at the ball and it sailed way above Mr Skelly's head.

'That time you kept your eye on the ball but you leaned back,' said Skenner.

'Yes,' Sken's dad called. 'Get your head over the ball.'

The next shot was low and fast. It flew straight past Mr Skelly into the goal.

Joe did it half-a-dozen times. He was still slipping but he was hitting the mark more often.

'Now try heading,' said Mr Skelly.

He lobbed the ball.

Joe raced in and *boom!* hit it hard. It flew quite a way.

'Ow!' yelled Joe because he still had a bump on his forehead from his miss in practice.

His friend's dad came up to him.

'You know something, Joe? You're better than you think. But you've got to believe you can do it.'

'What about me, Dad?' asked Skenner.

'Boggy pitches are a bit heavy for you, son, but I've watched Flowery before. They chase the ball all over the place. When they're worn out, that's when you should get going.'

Sken smiled and Joe thought hard. Mr Skelly knew what he was talking about. Joe didn't mind boggy pitches. And he was a good runner, even if he was clumsy. A plan was forming in his head about the game.

For the rest of the week, Joe practised with Sken and his dad, concentrating on his kicking. Sometimes Joe hit the ball straight. Sometimes it went wide again. But it seemed that the more he believed he could do it, the easier it was.

I'm not a joke now, thought Joe. Not a joke at all! But a practice wasn't like a real match and his boots were still not giving him enough grip.

He should have told his mum and dad about it straight away but, of course, he didn't. He was always shy to ask for things.

Finally, late on the night before the match, he could hold himself back no longer.

'Dad, I haven't got any proper football boots ...' he said.

'Ah,' said Dad. 'I might be able to help you there.'

At the words, Joe's heart leapt. New boots! he thought. He's got me some new boots! He must have got me them for Christmas, thought Joe. But now that I'm in an important match, he's giving them to me early.

Wonderful!

CHAPTER 3

Big boots

Dad went upstairs. Joe excitedly tried to watch the football preview on TV. He wasn't playing for Manchester United or Liverpool, of course, but he was part of it all now; part of the thrill.

His legs twitched with every kick on the screen. His head jerked with every centre. And all the time, his mind was racing ahead to his own great game the next morning, in his super new boots.

It was ages before his dad came downstairs again. He plonked a gigantic pair of shiny black boots in front of Joe.

As he stared at them, the boy felt as if someone had poured ice into his brain.

The boots were awful!

'Good, eh?' said his dad.

Joe found it hard to speak. He had never seen anything like them before.

They weren't low-cut and bendy, soft or supple. They had big, hard square toes, great big long studs and they were high at the ankle. They were his dad's old rugby boots, polished up.

Joe's mind was buzzing with disappointment. They had been good boots, quality boots. And they were his size. Joe's feet were enormous for his age. But he could imagine what everyone at school would say.

'They're …,' he finally gasped, 'exactly my size.'

At least I won't slip, he thought, the studs are like sharks' teeth! But he couldn't help thinking about the beauties in Ashton's windows. Real boots, not Noddy boots.

That night, he went to bed early but he didn't sleep much.

The wind moaned outside and Barney, his dog, moaned at the end of the bed. Dad coughed next door and Mum snored. He wouldn't have slept much anyway, because he was so terrified of being late.

He woke at 1.17, 2.49, 3.27, 3.43, 4.55. The numbers jumped off the big face of his digital clock. Then 10.40! Ahhh!!!!

He leapt up.

This time he had nodded off. He grabbed the clock. 6.03! 10.40 had been only a dream. At eight, breakfast time, it was raining like mad.

'Might get called off, Joe,' suggested his mum.

'Nay, Mother, it's not like cricket,' said his dad. 'Takes a lot to stop football.'

Joe checked his kit for the tenth time. He put his boots at the very bottom of his holdall, well out of sight. He had decided to put them on when nearly everyone had left the changing room. Then people like Tank wouldn't make fun of him. Soon, it was time to set out.

'See you!' he said.

'Good luck!' said his mum giving him a kiss.

His dad had his coat on, ready for his morning deliveries. 'Want a lift to school?' he said. 'I hope to get down to watch you when I've done the trip to Eccles.'

'Okay,' said Joe.

As Dad's van carried him down the hill to school, Joe was thinking about the boots. If only … but no, he had to stop that kind of thinking. It doesn't matter about the boots, he told himself.

They'll be covered in mud in no time anyway. They'll grip. They'll kick. Think about the game.

Still, he couldn't help wondering what Tank was going to say.

'Good luck!' said his dad. 'See you later!'

As Joe walked along the school drive he shivered. Suddenly fright ran all over him.

He felt like running away – but then he'd have to come back on Monday to tell the team why he left them one short.

He couldn't back out now. He *had* to know if he had really improved. He walked slowly towards the school.

Once inside, Joe changed into the blue and white of Newton Hall. He felt pure joy when he pulled the shirt over his head. He was playing for the school.

Maybe he'd only ever play once but at least he could say, 'I played for Newton Hall.'

Sken was facing him. He, too, looked happy and surprised.

They both looked up at the same second and burst out laughing.

Sken jogged happily out. Nobody expected anything from him.

Now there was only Joe and Arthur, the man-mountain goalkeeper, left. The big boy always came out last.

He had a yellow T-shirt, knee pads, elbow pads, ankle bandages and a collection of a dozen lucky charms he always kept in the back of the net.

In the end, Joe could not delay any longer. He just had to bring out the monster boots.

Arthur goggled. 'By 'eck, Joe, them's atomic boots!' he grinned.

'My dad's.'

Arthur stood, picked up his lucky charms, his cap and his gloves. Then he gave Joe a little pat on the face with his huge hand.

'Come on, Joe! Let's have some fun, eh?'

And out they clattered into the cold.

CHAPTER 4

Mud pies

Outside, Tank and Eddy just stared at Joe's feet. Then they began braying like donkeys as they scoffed at his boots.

'Look at them,' roared Tank. 'Where did you get them, Jurassic Park?'

'No, Tank,' chuckled Eddy, 'they're not that new!'

Joe felt his ears going red but he said nothing.

When Tank had stopped sniggering, he spoke to Joe and Skenner. 'You two, just keep out of my way, okay?'

Then Mr Murphy told Joe to stay wide on the left. So out Joe stayed. Skenner joined him. It was easier to avoid the clogging mud there.

Tank met Mark Bentley, the other captain, in the middle of the swamp. Mr Murphy tossed for ends, Mark called 'heads'. It wasn't his lucky day.

'We'll play with the tide,' laughed Tank, pointing at the mud.

'Don't get smart with me, Torkington!' snapped Mr Murphy, who wasn't in the mood for jokes. He turned to the other lad. 'Okay. You choose.'

'Hang on, you can't do that, sir! I won the toss!' Tank was purple now.

'And I'm the ref!'

Tank looked up at Mr Murphy's grim face and knew he couldn't win.

Flowery kicked off.

And so began a terrible game of football on a terrible day. The ball soon became a great leaden Christmas pudding that nobody, not even Tank, could kick more than a few metres.

Joe and Skenner never found out if they could or couldn't move it. They hardly even saw the ball. Nobody bothered to pass it to them at all.

To start with, everybody kept their positions. But soon there was almost a scrum round the ball. Only the two keepers plus Skenner and Joe kept clear.

Mud splattered in every direction. In the first ten minutes, there wasn't one shot at either goal.

Arthur started picking his nose in boredom. The other goalie was throwing mud pies at the goalposts to keep warm.

In no time at all, Flowery's canary-coloured shirts were yellowy-black and all Newton's players were blacky-blue – except the two outcasts on the wing, that is.

Finally, just on the stroke of half-time, Joe had a chance.

The ball flew behind the Flowery goal off a defender's slippery boot. Corner! On Joe's side.

At once, Eddy Morgan ran from the other wing to take it.

'It's my kick!' protested Joe.

'Get out of my way. You're not mucking this one up!' Eddy snapped.

Joe backed off. Splat! When Eddy hit the ball, it sounded like a wet cabbage. The ball squirted less than five metres before it stopped.

Eddy fell over backwards and slid along on his bottom. Everyone collapsed with laughter.

A Flowery defender thumped the ball out again.

Corner, again.

Eddy squelched into the middle with his shorts dangling down to his knees, like a wet nappy.

'You take it, Noddy Big Boots!' he sneered.

Joe put the ball on a little pile of mud, like a golf tee. He stepped back. Five paces, ten.

One-two-three-four … Joe ran in hard at the ball and whacked it with his left foot. It went zooming across the middle. The keeper came out but it skidded off his fingers and out of play on the far side.

The others goggled at where the ball had gone.

Mr Murphy blew for half-time. Tank said nothing.

CHAPTER 5

Runaround or hero?

At half-time, as they sucked their oranges, Joe looked hopefully for his dad but he was nowhere to be seen.

Joe and Sken huddled together.

'They're never going to pass to us, you know. I don't want to hang around on the wing any longer,' said Joe.

'Yes ...' but before Sken could say anything more, a mud ball splatted into his back.

Tank stood glowering. Mr Murphy was over on the other side of the pitch talking to Flowery's teacher.

'What was that for?' Sken gave Tank a hard look.

'It was to tell you that I'm fed up with you two wandering around like sheep on the wing whilst we do all the work.'

'So?' asked Joe.

'Help the defence!' snapped Tank.

'I'll think about it,' said Joe.

Tank took a step forward. Then he gave Joe a dirty look and stalked off. Joe noticed that Mr Murphy was coming over.

'You two,' said the teacher, 'help the defence. There doesn't seem to be much doing out in the middle.'

Joe groaned inside. He wanted to help the team but he saw no sense in going even further back. Arthur hadn't had one shot to save.

However, he did as he was told. He went back to the edge of the pond in front of Arthur's goal. Sken joined him.

The second half began. And, at first, Joe had nothing to do. The ball was still stuck around the centre circle where Tank and the other boys flopped about like elephants in a water hole. Then, ten minutes from the end, there was danger.

Arthur had booted the ball out but it went nowhere.

The goal was empty. The big Newton keeper was bogged down and the ball bounced just in front of Mark Bentley, the Flowery striker, who wound up a long-range shot.

B-Boom! The great shot sailed up and up over Arthur's head.

Then, it powered down and down and down, to come whizzing at Joe as he ran backwards to defend the open goal.

He had no time to think.

He just flung himself upwards and backwards like a dolphin.

Whumph! The ball smashed into his head like a brick and zoomed away towards the goal.

'Oooooo!' There was a great shout. Joe hardly dared look.

Where was the ball?

Was it behind him in the back of the net? No! The bar was twanging but the net was empty. He glanced down the field. Arthur was booting the ball out to Eddy on the wing.

Arthur waddled back to his goal like a huge bear. He patted Joe on the back.

'Great stop, Big Man! What a header!'

Others shouted, too, but Tank stared silently. Suddenly, Joe felt alive.

He could feel his face burning red and the pain in his head. 'Play back,' 'Leave it alone,' 'Do this, do that!' He was sick of it. Okay, he thought. Now it's my turn! Now, I'll play my game.

He started to go for everything. Suddenly everyone seemed to be moving in slow-motion. But the truth was that the others were very tired.

Joe could run and he hadn't done much to wear himself out.

'Ten minutes, lads! Hang on!' yelled the Flowery teacher. 'And watch that big kid! He's walking all over you!'

Suddenly, Joe was everywhere, a magnet for the ball. Tank stopped sulking and was up there with him.

They set up a chance to score but Tank's shot wasn't strong enough. It beat the keeper but stuck on the line in the mud. Now, it was Tank's turn to have a red face. If only it had been my shot, thought Joe.

By this time, Flowery were as mobile as garden gnomes and Newton Hall weren't much better. Tank and Joe battled on.

But there was still no goal. The match was starting to look like a 0-0 draw.

Then, in the last minute, Newton had a free kick on the edge of the Flowery penalty area.

People started to mark each other. Joe ran up to take the kick but Tank shook his head. 'No chance!' he called. 'This one's mine.'

Joe charged into the middle but Sken shouted to him.

'No, Joe, they've left a gap at the back!'

Joe realized that his friend was right. He took up a position beyond all the defenders and a little way out towards the wing.

Just as the ball was being placed, Joe started to have dreams of glory again. Then he thought, No, No! Stop it, stop this rubbish, Joe! Concentrate!

Tank thundered in for his moment of glory. *Thud!* He had meant to shoot – instead, the ball squirted sideways off his boot right across the face of the goal.

Over came the ball, flying like a great spotty, slimy cannonball straight at Joe.

The rest of the players were stranded, stiff scarecrows in the sludge of the penalty area.

Joe and his great boots stood alone, ten metres out.

'Hit it!' Joe's dad's voice cut the air, as Joe gave the ball a mighty thump with his right boot. Away it zoomed like a greasy pinball, through attackers and defenders alike, into the top corner of the net.

'Yehhhh!' Newton were shouting and racing at Joe, dragging him, slapping him on the back.

'Great goal, Joe!'

'A belter, Joe!'

No insults now! He tried to speak but his mind was all numb.

'You all right?' asked Mr Murphy as Joe counted his bruises.

But Joe didn't reply. Suddenly he was racing like mad towards his own goal.

Newton Hall were so tired that they had hardly gone beyond the half-way line. They thought the game was over.

But there was a great muddy gap between them and Arthur, the big goalie. Mark Bentley had spotted this and when Flowery kicked off, Craig Johnson, another Flowery player, booted the ball past the Newton team for Mark to chase after.

Danger! Mark was stomping. Arthur was lumbering. Sken was slithering. Joe gritted his teeth. It was a close race for the ball.

Mark and Joe got to it at the same time but Joe's big boot swept across Mark's toes. Wham! Out of play went the ball.

Down went the two players.

Then Mr Murphy blew for time and Newton Hall team jumped in the air shouting. Yehhh!!! Made it!!!!!!

Joe and Mark lay like black starfish in the mud.

'Well played!' said Mark.

'You too,' replied Joe.

Then Joe found himself being hauled to his feet. It was Tank! Joe wondered what he was going to say.

The two big boys were face to face but Tank didn't look him in the eye at first. Instead, he looked at the ground, red-faced. Then he looked up at Joe and gave him a little punch on the arm. 'Sorry, Joe!' he said.

Then it was Eddy's turn to say something to Joe.

'That goal was a cracker! I always knew you were a good 'un!'

As they all walked into the school, Mr Murphy came up and added his praise.

Finally, Joe's dad came up too.

'Well, son, you made it,' he said.

'Me, Skenner and your boots,' laughed Joe.

About the author

I spent most of my
football life as a defender.
However, my biggest thrill
came on one icy January
day in Manchester. That
day I scored my dream
goal from way outside
the penalty area.

   As the ball crashed in, I felt the way
strikers, big or small, black or white,
young or old, boy or girl, feel the world
over. It was a wonderful moment. My
team lost 5-1. I didn't score again that
season, but I'll always remember the way
the ball flew and the swish of the net.
Good luck, Joey Jones, wherever you are!